Backyard Bird Watchers

A Bird Watcher's Guide to
WOODPECKERS

By Grace Elora

Please visit our website, www.garethstevens.com. For a free color catalog of all our high-quality books, call toll free 1-800-542-2595 or fax 1-877-542-2596.

Cataloging-in-Publication Data

Names: Elora, Grace.
Title: A bird watcher's guide to woodpeckers / Grace Elora.
Description: New York : Gareth Stevens Publishing, 2018. | Series: Backyard bird watchers | Includes index.
Identifiers: ISBN 9781538203316 (pbk.) | ISBN 9781538203330 (library bound) | ISBN 9781538203323 (6 pack)
Subjects: LCSH: Woodpeckers—Juvenile literature.
Classification: LCC QL696.P56 E46 2018 | DDC 598.7'2—dc23

First Edition

Published in 2018 by
Gareth Stevens Publishing
111 East 14th Street, Suite 349
New York, NY 10003

Copyright © 2018 Gareth Stevens Publishing

Designer: Laura Bowen
Editor: Therese Shea

Photo credits: Cover, p. 1 (woodpecker) Rafal Szozda/Shutterstock.com; cover, pp. 1–32 (paper texture) javarman/Shutterstock.com; cover, pp. 1–32 (footprints) pio3/Shutterstock.com; pp. 4–29 (note paper) totallyPic.com/Shutterstock.com; pp. 4–29 (photo frame, tape) mtkang/Shutterstock.com; p. 4 Hatchapong Palurtchaivong/Shutterstock.com; p. 5 Vishal shinde/Shutterstock.com; p. 7 (main) Tom Reichner/Shutterstock.com; p. 7 (inset) Andrea Izzotti/Shutterstock.com; p. 8 Arr4/Wikimedia Commons; p. 9 (hairy woodpecker) Tm/Wikimedia Commons; p. 9 (ivory-billed woodpecker) FunkMonk/Wikimedia Commons; p. 9 (pileated woodpecker) Howcheng/Wikimedia Commons; p. 9 (acorn woodpecker and red-headed woodpecker) Helmy oved/Wikimedia Commons; p. 9 (red-bellied woodpecker) Ken Thomas/Wikimedia Commons; p. 11 (male) Matt Cuda/Shutterstock.com; p. 11 (female) Jim Nelson/Shutterstock.com; p. 15 Brent Barnes/Shutterstock.com; p. 17 Neil Petersen/EyeEm/Getty Images; pp. 19, 25 rck_953/Shutterstock.com; p. 21 Tom Reichner/Shutterstock.com; p. 23 FotoRequest/Shutterstock.com; p. 27 Jean-Edouard/Shutterstock.com; p. 29 Kellis/Shutterstock.com.

All rights reserved. No part of this book may be reproduced in any form without permission in writing from the publisher, except by a reviewer.

Printed in the United States of America

CPSIA compliance information: Batch #CS17GS: For further information contact Gareth Stevens, New York, New York at 1-800-542-2595.

CONTENTS

Knock-Knock Mystery 4
Waiting for Woodpeckers. 6
Smile, Woodpecker! 8
Spotted! 10
Where They Live 12
Hard Heads 14
Why All the Noise? 16
The Nest 18
Eager for Eggs 20
They're Here! 22
Out and About 24
Helpful or Harmful? 26
Sticking Together 28
Glossary 30
For More Information 31
Index 32

Words in the glossary appear in **bold** type the first time they are used in the text.

KNOCK-KNOCK MYSTERY

Funny Birds?
What bird is the best at knock-knock jokes?
A woodpecker!

4

I got this journal for my birthday. I'm going to use it to remember what happens. The funniest thing happened today! I heard someone knocking. I answered the door, but no one was there. I sat down and then heard it again: "Knock-knock-knock!"

I ran to the door. Again, no one was there! I thought my neighbor Toni was playing a trick on me when I heard the knocking again. I looked up and saw a bird pecking on a tree—a woodpecker!

Woodpeckers get their name from their actions. They peck at the bark on trees.

WAITING FOR WOODPECKERS

What Woodpeckers Eat

mostly bugs
fruits
acorns
nuts
sap
seeds

I told my sister Kim about the woodpecker. She's in a bird-watching club. She was really excited because she's never seen a woodpecker up close. We sat in the yard to watch for the bird.

Kim told me a few reasons why woodpeckers knock on trees with their beak. One is that they're looking for food. They eat bugs that live in trees. They can hear the bugs under the bark. Pecking is a way to get at them!

Some woodpeckers eat tree sap. Sap is a sticky matter that carries nutrients, water, and other important things throughout the tree.

tree sap

SMILE, WOODPECKER!

Gotcha!
This bird matches Kim's photo.

downy woodpecker

Finally, the woodpecker showed up. It started pecking on the tree. Kim took a picture of it with her phone. She says there are 180 species, or kinds, of woodpeckers!

Different woodpeckers live in different areas of the world. Kim showed me a bunch of photos online of different woodpeckers that live where we live in the United States. We'll be able to find out the species of the woodpecker in our yard by matching the bird's markings to one of these.

hairy woodpecker

ivory-billed woodpecker

pileated woodpecker

acorn woodpecker

red-bellied woodpecker

red-headed woodpecker

Here are some woodpeckers that live in the United States.

SPOTTED!

What Does It Mean?

downy = covered with soft feathers

You can see that the bird on the left has a red spot on its head. The rest of its body is black and white. It looks like it has white spots on its wings. It's a male downy woodpecker! Female downy woodpeckers don't have the red spot on their head.

Downy woodpeckers are pretty common in the United States, but they're the smallest woodpeckers here. They only grow to be about 6.5 inches (16.5 cm) long. Their wingspan is almost 12 inches (30 cm).

male

female

Some female woodpeckers have red heads, but not the female downy woodpecker.

WHERE THEY LIVE

Tongue Twister (Say it fast!)

How much wood could a woodpecker peck if a woodpecker could peck wood?

We live in a temperate part of the United States. That means it doesn't get too hot or too cold here. Downy woodpeckers like this kind of weather.

They live in places where there are **deciduous** trees, too. They like forests and **orchards**, like where we picked apples this year. But they also like towns and city parks—and yards like ours! Downy woodpeckers are smaller, so they might be found in bushes, too. They're happy wherever they can find bugs to eat.

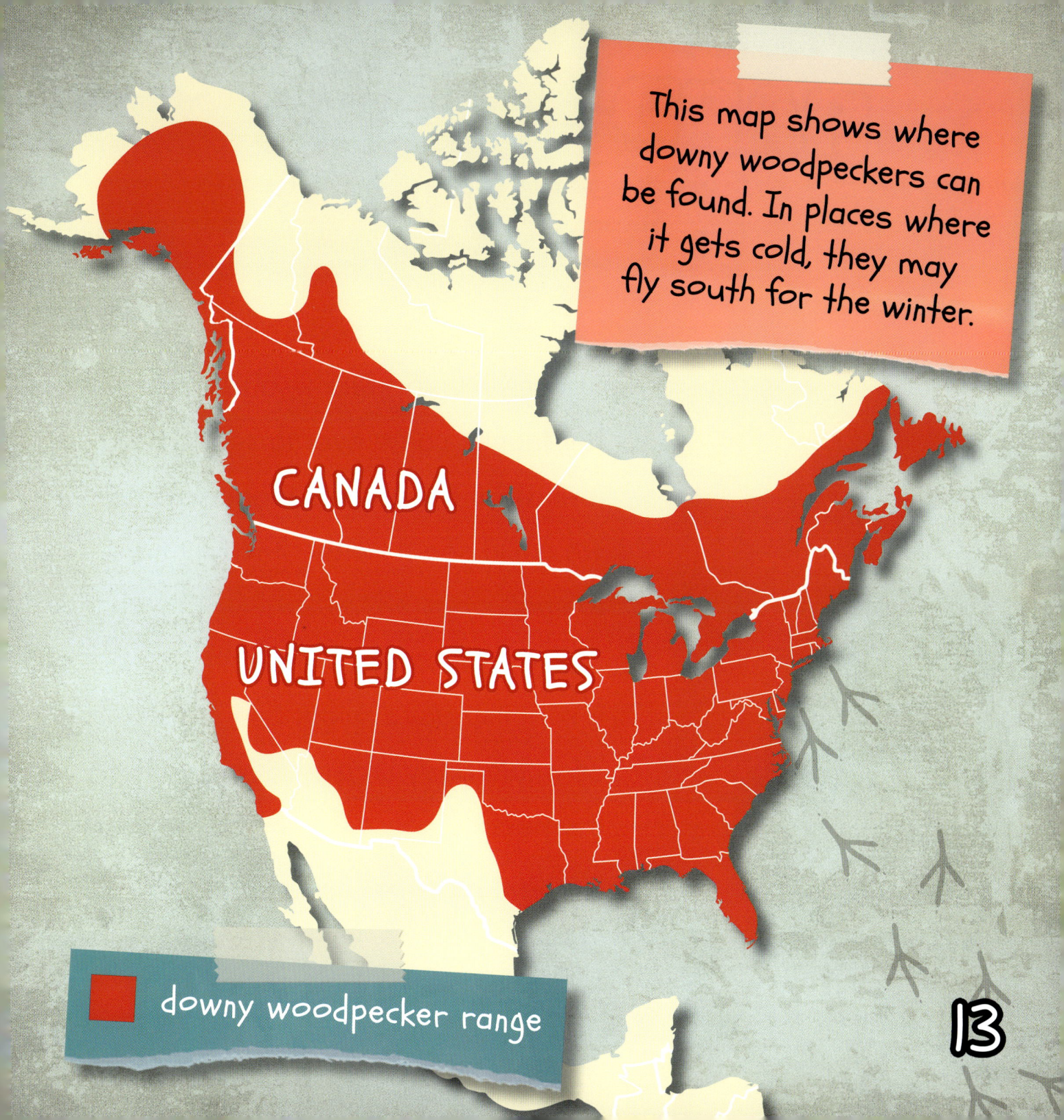

HARD HEADS

Crazy!

Woodpeckers have an inner eyelid to keep their eyeballs from popping out when they peck!

Kim told her bird-watching club about the woodpecker, and a few of her friends came over to see it. Her friend Cal brought his **binoculars** so we could see it better. It wasn't hard to spot!

As the bird pecked at the bark, it kept its back straight and leaned its whole body in. It's crazy how loud the pecking can be! Kim told me that woodpeckers have spongelike bone in their head. So, when they knock their beak against the hard wood, their brain doesn't rattle too much!

WHY ALL THE NOISE?

I found out something interesting from Kim's friend Cal. He said that woodpeckers don't knock loudly when they're looking for bugs. They actually do that quietly. When they're pecking loudly, they're calling to other woodpeckers.

Woodpeckers don't sing like many other kinds of birds do. Their pecks are their way of **communicating**. They tap to tell other males to get out of the territory. They tap to scare away predators. They also tap to draw **mates**.

How Many Times?!

Woodpeckers tap around 8,000 to 12,000 times a day!

When woodpeckers are trying to communicate, they find a wood surface that makes a loud sound so the noise travels far.

THE NEST

Hidden Home

Sometimes woodpeckers hide the entrance to a woodpecker nest with plants or fungus.

Today, I found out another reason why woodpeckers peck. We heard noise in the backyard and saw a female downy woodpecker tapping on a dead tree. She was making a hole. Later, I saw a male doing the same thing. I guessed they were mates making a place to put their nest! Kim says the hole in the tree is probably lined with wood chips.

Now we have a new place to watch each day. And there will be baby woodpeckers soon!

Both male and female downy woodpeckers make a cavity, or hole, in a dead tree to build their nest. It can take 3 weeks!

19

EAGER FOR EGGS

Where to Look

Nests are usually high—12 to 30 feet (3.7 to 9 m) from the ground.

While I'm waiting to see woodpecker chicks, I'm doing **research** on them. It's hard to see what's going on so high up a tree!

It's been fun learning facts from Kim. I found out facts online to tell her, too. I told her that downy woodpecker mothers lay three to six white eggs at a time. Each egg is less than 1 inch (2.5 cm) long. She told me the mother keeps the eggs warm for about 12 days. Then, they **hatch**!

The entrance to the nesting hole might only be 1 inch (2.5 cm) wide, but it can be 1 foot (30 cm) deep. It has to hold the mother and her babies.

THEY'RE HERE!

Today was an awesome day! We saw the woodpecker chicks poke their heads out of the hole in the tree. It was so cute! Cal was here so we used his binoculars to see what was going on.

We saw the woodpecker parents flying back and forth a lot and knew something was going on. They were bringing their babies food. While the baby woodpeckers are in the nest, they're called nestlings. And these nestlings eat a lot!

Stay Warm!

When woodpecker babies first hatch, they have no feathers and their eyes are closed.

Here's a picture of a woodpecker father feeding his babies!

OUT AND ABOUT

Not in the Nose!

Woodpeckers have feathers over their nose—so bits of wood don't get stuck in there!

The woodpecker chicks stay close to the nest growing their feathers and getting fed for about 3 weeks. Then, they start to follow their parents around. They learn how to fly and how to find food. Now, they're called fledglings.

Fledglings stick around their parents for another few weeks and then fly off to find their own territory. Woodpeckers that live in warm places may have another group of babies. In the fall, parents may separate to look for food in different places.

A downy woodpecker father feeds his fledgling. He sticks the food way back in its mouth!

HELPFUL OR HARMFUL?

Woodpeckers can do harm to trees while they're pecking thousands of times a day. Farmers who grow fruit trees really don't like these birds. And people who grow trees in order to sell wood don't like them, either. They do things such as put tape or nets over the holes the birds make to keep them from coming back.

But usually, woodpeckers are only looking for bugs in trees that are **infested** anyway. Woodpeckers eat the bugs that can harm trees, so that's helpful!

Sticky!

Woodpeckers use a sticky tongue to get bugs!

Acorn woodpeckers make holes in trees to store a favorite treat: acorns! These birds are mostly found on the West Coast.

STICKING TOGETHER

When woodpeckers are looking for food in winter, they sometimes join flocks of other bird species. This helps keep them safe from predators such as hawks, cats, and snakes. Downy woodpeckers like eating from **suet** feeders, so Kim and I bought one to put in our backyard.

It's been fun watching these cool birds. Kim's club made me a special member so I can learn more about birds as they do. Now, I'm a birder, too!

Attract a Woodpecker!

Downy woodpeckers eat black oil sunflower seeds, millet, peanuts, and chunky peanut butter. Draw one to your backyard!

GLOSSARY

binoculars: a tool that you hold up to your eyes and look through to see things that are far away

communicate: to give or receive information through noise, writing, or movement

deciduous: having leaves that fall off every year

fungus: a living thing that often looks like a plant but has no flowers and lives on dead or dying things

hatch: to come out of an egg

infest: to be in a place in large numbers

mate: one of two animals that come together to make babies

millet: a type of grass grown for its seeds, which are used as food

nutrient: something that plants, animals, and people need to live and grow

orchard: a place where people grow fruit trees

research: careful study that is done to find out something new

skull: the bones that form the head and face of a person or animal

suet: a type of hard fat that people mix with seeds, nuts, and fruit and feed to birds

FOR MORE INFORMATION

Books

Carr, Aaron. *Woodpeckers.* New York, NY: AV2 by Weigl, 2016.

Sayre, April Pulley. *Woodpecker Wham!* New York, NY: Henry Holt and Company, 2015.

Waxman, Laura Hamilton. *Pileated Woodpeckers: Insect-Hunting Birds.* Minneapolis, MN: Lerner Publications, 2016.

Websites

Downy Woodpecker
www.audubon.org/field-guide/bird/downy-woodpecker
Woodpeckers don't sing, but listen to their calls on this site.

Woodpeckers
www.defenders.org/woodpeckers/basic-facts
Read about different kinds of woodpeckers.

Publisher's note to educators and parents: Our editors have carefully reviewed these websites to ensure that they are suitable for students. Many websites change frequently, however, and we cannot guarantee that a site's future contents will continue to meet our high standards of quality and educational value. Be advised that students should be closely supervised whenever they access the Internet.

INDEX

acorn woodpeckers 27

babies 18, 21, 22, 23, 24

bark 5, 6, 14

beak 6, 14

bugs 6, 12, 16, 26

chicks 20, 22, 24

communicating 16, 17

eggs 20

eyelids 14

fathers 23, 25

feathers 10, 22, 24

females 10, 11, 18, 19

fledglings 24, 25

harm 26

heads 10, 11, 14, 22

helpful 26

males 10, 16, 18, 19

mates 16, 18

mother 20, 21

nestlings 22

nests 18, 20, 22, 24

sap 6, 7

skulls 15

species 8, 28

wingspan 10

winter 13, 28